All About

Weddings

All About Weddings

Ellen Bell

DUNDURN PRESS
TORONTO

Editor: Edward Butts
Copy editor: Barry Jowett
Design: Erin Mallory
Printer: Transcontinental

Library and Archives Canada
Cataloguing in Publication

Bell, Ellen
    All about weddings / written by
Ellen Bell.

ISBN 978-1-55002-885-0

    1. Weddings--Miscellanea. 2.
Weddings--History. 3. Marriage
customs and rites. I. Title.

HQ745.B46 2008   395.2'2
C2008-903785-5

        1   2   3   4   5
      12   11   10   09   08

Conseil des Arts   Canada Council
du Canada   for the Arts

ONTARIO ARTS COUNCIL
CONSEIL DES ARTS DE L'ONTARIO

Canadä

We acknowledge the support of
The Canada Council for the Arts
and the Ontario Arts Council for
our publishing program. We also
acknowledge the financial support
of the Government of Canada
through the Book Publishing
Industry Development Program
and The Association for the Export
of Canadian Books, and the
Government of Ontario through the
Ontario Book Publishers Tax Credit
program, and the Ontario Media
Development Corporation.

J. Kirk Howard, President

Printed and bound in Canada.

www.dundurn.com

Dundurn Press	Gazelle Book Services Limited	Dundurn Press
3 Church Street, Suite 500	White Cross Mills	2250 Military Road
Toronto, Ontario, Canada	High Town, Lancaster,	Tonawanda, NY
M5E 1M2	England LA1 4XS	U.S.A. 14150

All About

Weddings

Contents

Preface

Say the word "wedding" and, for most people, the same pictures will immediately come to mind. The nervous groom and his best man wait with a clergyman at the altar of a church in front of a congregation of family and friends. An organist plays "The Wedding March," and the bride — dressed in a beautiful white gown — walks down the aisle arm in arm with her proud father. In front of them is a little flower girl and possibly a little boy, who is the ring bearer. Following them are the bridesmaids, also wearing lovely gowns. They are escorted by the ushers. All of the males in the wedding party are formally dressed. At the altar, the father of the bride passes his daughter over to the groom. There is a ceremony in which the couple exchanges vows, the groom places a ring on the bride's finger, and the clergyman pronounces them man and wife. The groom kisses the bride, and women in the congregation wipe their eyes. Then everyone goes outside for photographs and showers of confetti before they get into cars for a horn-honking drive to the reception hall.

Of course, not every wedding fits this picture. But for every familiar ritual mentioned here — and many others — there is an origin in history and lore. Wedding ceremonies and the customs that precede and follow them are well steeped in tradition and superstition. In this book we look at some of the facts and legends that surround those two famous words: "I do."

Going to the Chapel

What is a wedding?

A wedding is a ceremony — whether it is simple or elaborate, civil or religious — in which two people are joined together in matrimony. Usually the wedded partners are male and female, but in many jurisdictions same-sex marriages are now legal and becoming more commonplace.

What is the origin of the word "wedding"?

The old Anglo-Saxon word *wedd* meant "pledge." The pledge in this case wasn't between the bride and groom.

Rather, it was the groom's pledge to the bride's father that he would care for her, and of course, pay the father for her. (This is also the origin of the word "wages.")

When was the first wedding?

The first recorded weddings took place in ancient Egypt. The bride simply had to move into the groom's house to be considered legally married, but the event was usually marked with a celebration. Anthropologists have concluded that, in pre-historic cultures all over the world, marriages were performed in many ways, sometimes with much ritual and sometimes with none at all. Hunter-gatherer societies probably didn't have as much time or as many resources to celebrate weddings as did agricultural societies.

Why did ancient peoples have weddings?

In ancient times it was important that marriages be both legally recognized and acceptable to the gods. A wedding was a way of announcing to one and all that a man and woman were now husband and wife. It solidified political connections, ownership of land and other property, military alliances, and the legitimacy of children. It also helped prevent incest in places where such close family relationships were not acceptable. Wedding ceremonies usually asked the gods to bless the union with prosperity and children.

Who arranged weddings in ancient times?

Weddings were usually arranged by the parents of the bride and groom, often when the future spouses were still small children. Sometimes a wedding was arranged by the prospective groom and the father of the prospective bride. Romantic love usually had nothing to do with it, and the bride rarely had any say in the matter.

Ten Countries in Which Most Marriages Are Still Arranged

- Afghanistan
- Albania
- Algeria
- Azerbaijan
- Bahrain
- Bangladesh
- Cambodia
- Gambia
- India
- Indonesia

What was "marriage by proxy"?

This generally happened among royalty and the nobility. If for some reason one of the partners could not be at the wedding in person, the marriage ceremony was nonetheless carried out with the other partner. This could happen in time of war or for political reasons. In 1625, King Charles I of England was married by proxy to Princess Henrietta Maria of France. The ceremony was held at the door of

Another Guide for the
Best Time of Year
for a Wedding

Married when the year is new,
he'll be loving, kind, and true.
When February birds do mate,
you wed nor dread your fate.
If you wed when March winds blow,
joy and sorrow both you'll know.
Marry in April when you can,
joy for maiden and for man.
Marry in the month of May,
and you'll surely rue the day.
Marry when June roses grow,
over land and sea you'll go.
Those wed in August be,
many a change is sure to see.
Marry in September's shrine,
your living will be rich and fine.
If in October you do marry,
love will come but riches tarry.
If you wed in bleak November,
only joy will come, remember.
When December snow falls fast,
marry and true love will last.

Notre Dame Cathedral without Charles being present. Later the princess went to England and she and Charles were married again at the door of Canterbury Cathedral.

What was the difference between a "dowry" and a "bride price"?

Who had to pay what to whom before a wedding could occur varied from place to place. A "dowry" was money or valuable property a bride took to the marriage. It was usually provided by her father. A "bride price" was the money or property the bridegroom had to pay to the bride's family for her hand in marriage. If the bridegroom had no money, he could sometimes pay the bride price with his labour.

Why is June supposed to be a lucky month for weddings?

June was named for the Roman goddess Juno. She was the faithful wife of Jupiter, chief god in the Roman pantheon. Juno was also the patron goddess of women. Marital unions that took place in her month were believed to have her blessing, and would therefore be joyous and fruitful. On the other hand, May weddings were considered unlucky. The goddess Maia was the wife of Vulcan, the god of fire. Marriages that took place in her month were liable to be "volcanic" and unhappy.

What, according to old folklore, is the best day of the week for a wedding?

By the time of the Christian era, Sundays were out, because that was the Lord's Day. Otherwise:
- Monday for health
- Tuesday for wealth
- Wednesday best of all
- Thursday for losses
- Friday for crosses
- Saturday no luck at all

What is the largest wedding on record?

In 1995 at the Olympic Stadium in Seoul, South Korea, Sun Myung Moon of the Holy Spirit Association of the Unification of World Christianity married 35,000 couples. Another 350,000 were joined in wedlock by satellite link.

Where does the greatest number of weddings occur?

Las Vegas, Nevada, is the wedding ceremony capital of the world. The city's one hundred chapels handle 8,400 marriages a month. That works out to one wedding every five minutes and seventeen seconds.

What were the five steps to marriage?

- legal contract
- the spousal (engagement)
- a public proclamation
- the public ceremony
- consummation

Why are wine, salt, and bread significant in many ethnic weddings?

Wine represents the joy of marriage. Salt represents the tears that all married couples shed at one time or another. Bread represents the labour the couple must share to support themselves and their children.

Three Celebrity Weddings That Took Place in Las Vegas

- Elvis Presley and Priscilla Beaulieu
- Bruce Willis and Demi Moore
- Richard Gere and Cindy Crawford

All ended in divorce.

Why do Christian weddings take place in a church?

Christians consider marriage a sacred institution. A wedding in a church asks God to bless the union. Originally the weddings were held outside the church doors. Once the ceremony was completed, the wedding party followed the priest inside to hear mass.

What was a Besom wedding?

In rural Britain, a Besom wedding was a form of trial marriage involving a birch besom — a broom made with twigs or brushy plants. This was also said to be the kind of broom favoured by witches. The besom was laid at the threshold of the house the couple would inhabit, and the bride and groom jumped over it in turn, in front of witnesses. They were then considered married. If at the end of a year the husband and wife were happy with each other, they would have a proper wedding. However, if one or both partners should be unhappy with the marriage, they could annul it by jumping over the besom backwards. If there was a child, caring for it was the man's responsibility.

What is the origin of the word "spouse"?

The origin of the word has been lost, but it did not always mean "husband" or "wife," as it does today. At one time a spouse was a person who had entered into a promise of marriage.

Why is it traditional for the father of the bride to pay for the wedding?

In weddings going back to the earliest times, the bride was expected to bring a large amount of property or money — called a "dowry" or "marriage portion" — to the marriage. This was her share of her father's estate, and it was given to the groom's father. He often used it to provide a dowry for his own daughter. It was also meant to be an insurance fund for the bride in case her husband died. The dowry eventually became unfashionable, but the responsibility of paying for the wedding remained with the bride's father, since the groom was taking over the cost of providing for the daughter.

What is a "shotgun wedding"?

This American colloquialism refers to a situation in which a young woman becomes pregnant out of wedlock, and a wedding takes place with her father standing behind the man responsible with a loaded shotgun. The groom either says "I do" or suffers the consequences. A wedding that is hastily arranged to avoid the embarrassment of out-of-wedlock pregnancy is still referred to as a shotgun wedding. However, with the decline of the negative stigma attached to pregnancy out of wedlock, such weddings are becoming rare.

What are "mail-order brides"?

In the nineteenth century, some women listed their names in catalogues and were chosen by men for marriage. Such women were often destitute, or were anxious to emigrate from their home countries to Canada, the United States, or Australia. In the western frontier regions of North America, the male population greatly outnumbered the females, and many men turned to the mail-order bride catalogues to find wives. There are still mail-order bride agencies through which women in Third World and developing countries seek husbands in developed nations. However, these agencies work through the internet rather than regular mail.

What is the origin of the expression "married in her shift"?

In England of old, if a man married a woman who had no dowry or estate, and he wanted to show that he would not be responsible for any debts she might owe, he would make her come to the wedding dressed only in her "shift" — a simple smock. The expression eventually came to be applied to any woman who was financially destitute at the time of her wedding.

Who were the youngest married couple on record?

In Bangladesh in 1986, an eleven-month-old boy was married to a three-month-old girl to settle their families' decades-old dispute over ownership of a farm.

What couple holds the record for the most times renewing their wedding vows?

An American couple, Lauren Lubeck Blair and David E. Hough Blair, formally renewed their wedding vows eighty-three times, most recently in Las Vegas, Nevada.

What countries have the lowest and highest marriage rates?

The Dominican Republic has the lowest marriage rate, at just two marriages per one thousand population. Antigua and Barbuda recorded the highest marriage rate, at 22.1 marriages per one thousand population.

Will You Marry Me?

Why is a young man trying to win a woman's love said to be "courting" her?

Wherever a sovereign lived and held state was known as court. The monarch's advisors, ministers, and various officials were his or her courtiers. When one was at court, and therefore in the presence of the monarch, one had to be on the best of behaviour — hence, the word "courtesy." Anyone wanting to gain royal favour had to do so through the courtiers, and this could mean laying on a lot of flattery. So, a young man paying courteous attention to a woman in hopes of winning her favour, and quite likely flattering her, was said to be "courting."

What was the origin of the word "woo"?

The origin of the word is obscure, but it probably comes from Old English. To "woo" a person means to court or make love. According to an old saying, "to woo is a pleasure in a young man, a fault in an old."

What is the origin of the word "fiancé/fiancée"?

It comes from the French word for betrothal, *fiancailles*. A male who is engaged to be married is a "fiancé," while the female is the "fiancée." The word is commonly used in the English-speaking world, but early in the twentieth century it was considered a coarse expression by high society.

Why is it customary for the man to "pop the question"?

From the earliest times it has been up to the male (or his parents) to make known his desire to take a wife. For the female to be seen to be "husband hunting" would be considered shameful. In many societies the man did not ask the woman if she would marry him; he asked her father. Later, as women gained more freedom, the would-be bride was allowed to choose her own husband, and her suitor asked the father for her hand strictly as a formality.

Why does the groom-to-be ask the father of the prospective bride for her hand in marriage?

Until very recently in history, women were considered property. A girl belonged to her father until she was married, at which time she became the property of her husband. When a girl married, her father lost the labour she provided in the house and on the farm. He was also surrendering a bloodline to another family. The father wanted to be assured that he would be compensated for this loss. He also wanted to be sure that his prospective son-in-law would provide for his daughter and be a worthy sire of his daughter's children.

Why does the man get down on one knee when he asks the woman to marry him?

The custom dates back to medieval times and the age of chivalry. Going down on one knee showed humility and subservience. According to the Knight's Code, women were to be respected at all times (at least, aristocratic ladies were). A gallant knight bent his knee only before God, his monarch, or his lady love.

What was the origin of the engagement ring?

The giving of engagement rings was an established custom

by the Middle Ages, but just when it began is not certain. In Shakespeare's time the rings were called "posey rings." "Posey" was a corruption of "poetry" and referred to the motto inscribed in the ring. Gimmal rings were also popular. Gimmal rings consisted of two or three interlocking rings, often with a central motif of two hands crossed over a heart. At the time of the betrothal, the rings would be ceremoniously broken apart over a bible, and the young man and woman would each receive a part. If there were three rings, the third part went to a witness. At the wedding, the pieces of the ring would be combined into one as the bride's wedding ring.

Who first gave his betrothed a diamond engagement ring?

The tradition that is such an expensive one for young men was started by Holy Roman Emperor Maximilian I in 1477. The emperor, who could afford such things, gave a diamond ring to Mary of Burgundy, a duchess to whom he had proposed marriage. Before that, the engagement ring didn't necessarily have to be a diamond. In A.D. 860, Pope Nicholas I decreed that a ring of value must be given as a statement of nuptial intent and that if the man called off the wedding, the jilted bride kept the ring. If the woman ended the engagement, she was to return the ring and be sent to a nunnery.

Eleven Words or Expressions Meaning Engaged or Engagement

- Betrothal
- Betrothment
- Espousal
- Troth (an Old English word for loyalty or truth)
- Marriage contract
- Handfasting
- Vow
- Plighted troth (or faith or love)
- Affianced
- Pledged
- Promised

What was a "philter"?

A philter was an aphrodisiac — a potion or charm that would help a person win the love of another person. A philter was most likely to be used by a woman with designs on a particular man. Many so-called "love potions" contained ingredients like honey and mandrake. However, the philter did not necessarily have to be something that was ingested. One charm called for the woman to go into a graveyard at night and remove a strip of skin from a man who had been buried for exactly nine days. That same night, she had to tie this around the arm or leg of the man she desired as he slept, but she had to remove it before he awakened. The man would then be under a spell and would love her forever.

What was a "wet bargain"?

This was a betrothal sealed with a kiss. The betrothal, as

a promise to marry, was taken very seriously and often required more than a mere handshake. It often took place in the doorway of a church, or at a local "betrothal stone." For one of the parties to back out of the agreement could have significant social consequences. According to the "wet bargain," if the engagement did not lead to marriage, the man had

> **QUICKIES**
> **Did you know ...**
>
> • that in medieval England women weren't allowed to ask men to marry them? However, February 29 wasn't recognized as an official day, therefore laws and statutes weren't upheld. On that day, women were equal to men and could ask men to marry them.

to return all of the gifts the woman had given him, but the woman had to return only half the gifts the man had given her. If there had been no kiss, both parties had to return all gifts.

How did unscrupulous men abuse the custom of betrothal?

Cads and scoundrels would woo young heiresses with promises of marriage, and once they got their hands on some of the money they would renege on the agreement. In England in 1753, Lord Hardwick's Marriage Act was made law to prevent such abuses.

What are "banns"?

Banns are a notice, usually given in church, of an approaching marriage. Banns would usually be read out on the three Sundays prior to the wedding. The English Book of Common Prayer prescribed the wording of the announcement: "I publish the Banns of Marriage between _____ and _____. If any of you know cause, or just impediment, why these two persons should not be joined together in Holy Matrimony, ye are to declare it." The most common reasons for anyone objecting to a marriage were: the couple were too closely related, or one or both were already married to someone else.

What was the origin of the custom of giving one's betrothed a lock of one's hair?

There were many superstitions involving hair, such as the belief that a witch could use a lock of hair to put a curse on the person the hair came from. To give one's betrothed a lock of hair was to show absolute trust. It meant that the person giving the hair delivered himself/herself body and soul to the recipient.

What was "bundling"?

In colonial America, if a young man paid a visit to the home of his betrothed on a cold winter evening, he might — with her parents' permission — bundle with her. That meant he could sleep next to her in her bed, but both he and she had to be well-bundled in clothing. There might also be a "bundling board" between them. This spared the young man a long, cold walk home. It also meant the girl's family didn't have to keep a fire roaring all night. In spite of the clothing and the bundling board, many a young woman who had bundled with her betrothed went to the altar already in a family way.

Here Comes the Bride

What is the origin of the word "bride"?

The word "bride" comes from an Old English word that means "cook." "Bridal" dates back to the twelfth century, and comes from "bride ale," a specially brewed beer that was served at weddings. Bride ale was a potent drink, so weddings could quickly become quite rowdy.

Why does the bride have a bridal shower?

The bridal shower is said to be a North American custom, but in recent years people in other countries have adopted the practice. Traditionally a friend or relative of the bride (frequently the person invited to be maid of honour) arranges the bridal shower. Originally only women attended bridal showers, but today they are often attended by men, too. The person hosting the shower serves food and drinks, and people bring gifts for the bride. These are usually the sort of items she will need to start a household, and lingerie. Sometimes there is a money tree, to which people clip gifts of cash.

Why are wedding-related items referred to as "bridal"?

The expressions "bridal feast," "bridal bed," and "bridal cake," among other bridal references, all date back to around 1200, when a wedding was a rather boisterous and bawdy affair. The word "bridal" comes from "bride-ale," which was the special beer brewed for the wedding and then sold to the guests to raise money for the newlyweds. Because of the bride-ale, weddings were generally quite rowdy until around the seventeenth century, when the church managed to get a grip on the whole thing.

What was "bidding"?

This was a custom in Wales and parts of England. On the eve of the wedding or on the wedding day, there would be a large gathering at which money and gifts were given to the betrothed couple. Every donation had to be recorded, because the couple had to return a gift of equal value to the donor — if the donor should so bid them. Food and drinks were sold, and the proceeds given to the couple.

Why does a bride have bridesmaids?

Today, bridesmaids dressed in lovely gowns contribute to a decorative formal wedding procession and to very attractive wedding pictures. Centuries ago, the bridesmaids were there to confuse evil spirits. The troublesome phantoms would not be sure which woman was the bride, and so would not know whom to work their mischief on. In some places the bride's maiden friends would stand at the door of her home to prevent the groom from entering and seeing her before the wedding. In Roman times a marriage required ten witnesses, which usually included female friends of the bride. In the nineteenth century the bridesmaids helped the bride dress for the wedding, and then they helped her undress for the marriage bed. In some places it was customary for the bride to have page boys instead of, or in addition to, bridesmaids.

Why do some brides have a flower girl?

A pretty little flower girl certainly enhances wedding photographs. In Old England, a flower girl walked at the head of the procession from the bride's home to the church, tossing petals. Flowers at weddings date back many centuries; it was believed the sweet fragrance of flowers kept away evil spirits, which is also why the bride carries a bouquet. In Greek and Roman times the bride carried herbs.

Why does a bride wear white?

In most European cultures, going back to the ancient Greeks, white is the colour of purity, virginity, and innocence. White is also the symbolic colour of joy. The ancient Greeks painted their bodies white on the evening of a wedding.

Where have colours other than white been tradition-al for bridal gowns?

In ancient Rome, brides

An Old English Rhyme about Weddings and Colours

Married in white,
you have chosen right
Married in red,
you'd better be dead
Married in yellow,
ashamed of the fellow
Married in blue,
your lover is true
Married in green,
ashamed to be seen
Married in black,
you'll wish yourself back
Married in pearl,
you'll live in a whirl
Married in pink,
your spirits will sink
Married in brown,
you'll live out of town
Married in grey,
you will go far away

usually wore yellow or blue. In Icelandic weddings, the bride wore black velvet. Green has been the traditional bridal colour in Norway, while in China the colour is red. During the Revolutionary War, American brides wore red as a sign of rebellion. In many instances the bride could not afford a wedding gown, and so just wore her best dress. In medieval Europe, among the nobility, the richness of a wedding gown's fabric and embroidery was more important than the colour.

What is the origin of the bridal veil?

There are several versions:

- It is a relic of ancient days when a man would throw a blanket over a woman's head and carry her off in bridal capture.
- It protected the bride from evil spirits and the evil eye.
- In arranged marriages, it hid the bride's face from the groom until it was too late for him to back out of the marriage.
- It is a leftover from the eastern practice of keeping all girls' faces covered until they were married.
- It is a throwback to Anglo-Saxon weddings, in which four men held a "care cloth" over the heads of the bride and groom.

In the nineteenth century it was considered good luck to have the veil put on the bride by a happily married man. It was considered extremely bad luck if the veil should be accidentally torn.

Why does a bride wear "Something old, something new, something borrowed, something blue"?

This rhyme has come down from Victorian England. Something old — a used article of clothing from a happily married woman (but not a widow). Something new — an unused article of clothing to transfer the good luck from the old article to the new bride. Something borrowed — an object made of gold, such as a ring. (Gold represented the sun, which was a symbol of luck and fertility.) Something blue — like white, blue was a symbol of purity. (The Virgin Mary is often shown dressed in blue.) Blue also represents the sky — the connection between the sun and the bride.

> **QUICKIES**
> **Did you know ...**
>
> • that the most expensive wedding dress on record was created by Helene Gailville, with jewels by Alexander Reza? The jewellery included diamonds mounted on platinum. The gown was displayed in March 1989 and was valued at $7.3 million.

How did Queen Victoria revolutionize weddings?

- She wore a simple white gown instead of a richly embroidered one.
- She wore a garland of orange blossoms on her head instead of a jeweled tiara.
- Her bouquet included myrtle.
- She wore a veil of Honiton lace. (The town of Honiton, England, was famous for its fine lace.)
- The music she chose for her wedding was "The Bridal March," composed by Richard Wagner for the opera *Lohengrin*. It is the "Here Comes the Bride" music heard at so many weddings today.
- Victoria's marriage to Prince Albert was unique among royal weddings in that the bride and groom were actually in love with each other. In fact, *she* had proposed to *him*!

Why does the bride toss her bouquet and the groom toss her garter?

At one time the bridesmaids and groomsmen tossed the bride and groom's stockings at the bride and groom. If a stocking landed on the target's head, it meant the person who had thrown it would be married within the year.

In days of yore, the bride's wedding dress was a symbol of good luck, and wedding guests would often grab at the bride, trying to tear off pieces. To avoid this, the bride would throw her bouquet to the unmarried female guests, and the groom would throw an article of her clothing, such as a garter, to the unmarried males. The individuals who caught these items would, supposedly, be the next to be married, though not necessarily to each other.

Who is the oldest bride on record?

The oldest known bride was 102-year-old Minnie Munro of Australia, who married eighty-three-year-old Dudley Reid on May 31, 1991.

Wedding Music in Other Countries

In Afghanistan, the traditional wedding song is called *Hoesta Boro* ("Walk Softly"). In Guyana, wedding celebrants sing *Queh Queh*, traditional Guyanese folk songs.

Who has been a bride in monogamous weddings the most frequently?

The most frequently married woman on record is Linda Lou Essex of Indiana, who married fifteen different men between 1957 and 1991. The marriages all ended in divorce.

The Lucky Man

What is the origin of the word "bridegroom"?

"Groom" comes from the Anglo Saxon word *guma*, which means "young man." A bridegroom was therefore a young man who was taking a bride. Traditionally, the bride is considered the most important person at a wedding; the bridegroom always seems to have a secondary role. The reason for this could be that the bride was entitled to one big day before entering into a life of subservience to her husband.

Why does the groom have a "best man"?

In a modern wedding the best man presents the groom

with the ring for the bride's finger. Like the bridesmaids, he also is included in pictures for the wedding album. In ancient times, when men went on raids to capture brides from neighbouring villages, the prospective groom took along his best friend as a swordsman who would fight off the girl's male relatives. In the Roman world the ten witnesses required at a wedding included several of the groom's male friends. The term "best man" did not come into use until the nineteenth century. Prior to that, the bridegroom's chief supporter at the wedding was called a "groomsman." The bridegroom could have more than one groomsman — friends or relatives who did the tasks now done by ushers.

What is the origin of the stag party?

The stag party, also called a bachelor party, is a twentieth-century invention. It is usually organized by the groom's best man, and is supposed to be the groom's

QUICKIES
Did you know ...

• that when English novelist Charles Dickens married Catherine Thompson Hogarth on April 2, 1836, he wanted his publisher, John Macrone, to be his best man? The bride, however, would not permit it. Macrone was married, and according to tradition the best man at a wedding was supposed to be unmarried. An ominous beginning, perhaps, for a marriage that was not very happy.

last opportunity to celebrate as a single man. Most stag parties involve alcohol and gambling, with a percentage of the money going to the groom to help pay for the honeymoon.

Why does the groom wear a boutonniere?

One source claims the colourful flower in the groom's lapel is a leftover from the days of chivalry, when a knight would proudly wear his lady-love's colours. However, it seems more likely that the boutonniere had its origin in the days when "wedding favours" such as flowers were distributed during and after the ceremony. The button hole for the boutonniere did not appear in lapels until the 1840s.

What is a "groom's cake"?

The groom's cake originated in the southern United States. The wedding cake, also called the "bride's cake," is eaten at the reception. The groom's cake is cut up and given to the guests to take home. If an unmarried girl puts the piece of cake under her pillow, she will supposedly dream about the man she will marry. The groom's cake is usually a fruitcake, and is not as beautifully decorated as the wedding cake. Usually the bride orders the groom's cake and has it shaped in a way that reflects the groom's personality: a car, a compass, etc. It is bad luck for the bride to let the groom see the groom's cake before the wedding, or to tell him what shape it is.

Why does the groom stand to the right of the bride?

This goes back to the age of chivalry. The groom stood to the right of the bride so that his right arm would be free to draw his sword, if necessary. The groomsmen were supposed to be ready to go into action if there was any kind of trouble at the wedding, but the groom had to show that he was ready to personally defend his bride and his honour.

Why does the groom traditionally wear a black tuxedo?

At one time the groom simply wore the best suit of clothes he owned to his wedding. In some places he wore a smock with a cross embroidered on it. After the wedding he put the smock away. It was not to be used again until he died and it became his burial shroud. For centuries, gentlemen of means got married in any colour *except* black, which was associated with death and considered bad luck.

In 1886 a millionaire named Pierre Lorillard wore a black, tailless evening jacket of his own design to a dinner at Tuxedo Park in New York. The fashion world was stunned. However, Lorillard alone must not be blamed for the much-hated tux. He got the idea from a friend named James Brown Potter. Potter had been in England, and got the design from the Prince of Wales (later King Edward VII). It became the suit a man was expected to wear on his wedding day. Today, however, many designs and colours are acceptable.

Why does the groom carry the bride over the threshold?

In ancient times the door of every home in a village had a raised board at the bottom to prevent the thresh (dried waste parts of grain) that littered the ground from being blown into the house. It was an easy thing to trip over. Tripping over the threshold the first time a person entered a house was considered bad luck. Since women were thought to be less coordinated than men, there was a great danger that the clumsy bride would trip over the threshold and bring ill fortune to the marriage. It was also bad luck to enter the house with the left foot first. A woman on her wedding day might be too emotionally distracted to remember such an important point, so the more emotionally composed man would carry her over the threshold to avoid calamity.

Why is it bad luck for the groom to see the bride before the wedding?

This superstition goes back to the time when most marriages were arranged by parents. If the groom-to-be saw the bride (whom he might never have met before) and didn't like her looks, he might back out of the wedding. Thus, he was not allowed to see her until he met her at the wedding, when he had no choice but to marry her.

What is the origin of the expression "tie the knot"?

There are two explanations. One says the expression came from India. In a Hindu wedding ceremony the groom would put a brightly coloured ribbon around the bride's neck. During the time it took to tie the ribbon into a knot, the bride's father could demand a better price for his daughter. But once the knot was completed, the bride became the groom's forever.

The other explanation says the expression comes from the Romans. The bride would wear a girdle that was tied in many knots, and the groom would have the duty of untying them when he undressed her.

Why does the groom at a Jewish wedding crush a glass with his foot?

Near the end of a Jewish wedding ceremony, after the vows have been made, wine is poured into a new glass over which a blessing is recited by the rabbi. After the couple drinks from the glass, it is placed on the ground and crushed by the groom's foot. This symbolizes the destruction of the Holy Temple in Israel and reminds guests that love is fragile. Those gathered shout "mazel tov" and the couple kisses.

Who was the oldest bridegroom on record?

The oldest known bridegroom was Harry Stevens, a 103-year-old American who married eighty-four-year-old Thelma Lucas on December 3, 1984.

What is the record for bigamous marriages?

On March 28, 1983, in Phoenix, Arizona, a man going by the name of Giovanni Vigliotto was convicted of 104 bigamous marriages. The weddings took place from 1949 to 1981 in twenty-seven American states and fourteen countries. He was sentenced to twenty-eight years in prison for fraud, another six years for bigamy, and fined $336,000.

Cakes and Rings and Wedding Things

What is the origin of the wedding cake?

The consumption of pastries and various kinds of bread at weddings goes back to the ancient Egyptians. The Greeks ate honey cakes, and the Romans actually threw sweet cakes at the bride. In medieval England wedding guests brought their own biscuits or scones to a wedding. These baked goods were placed in a pile. The higher the pile, the brighter the future for the married couple. The bride and groom would kiss over the stack of biscuits and scones. During the reign of King Charles II, a French chef visiting London found this custom of piling up pastry appalling. He created a three-tiered wedding cake that was encrusted with hardened white sugar and decorated with toys and figures. The cake was allegedly modeled after the spire of St. Bride's Church in London. The wedding cake was actually called "the bride's cake" until late in the nineteenth century. Sometimes there were two wedding cakes: one to be eaten, and the other to be broken over the bride's head for luck. Today the bride and groom usually cut the first piece of cake together, but in earlier times it might be the bride or groom alone, or an unmarried girl or a bachelor.

Who owns the most expensive piece of wedding cake?

In February 1998, in an auction at Sotheby's of New York, Benjamin and Amanda Yim bid $29,000 for a piece of cake left over from the wedding of the Duke and Duchess of Windsor.

What was the world's largest wedding cake?

In February 2008, executive pastry chef Lynn Mansel and a team of fifty-seven "pastry artists" constructed a giant cake for the New England Bridal Showcase at the Mohegan Sun Resort in Connecticut. The cake weighed 15,032 pounds, was seventeen feet high, and could provide slices of cake for 59,000 people.

How did Princess Elizabeth (later Queen Elizabeth II) out-do Queen Victoria in the matter of weddings?

Elizabeth Windsor, heiress to the throne of England, married Philip Mountbatten on November 20, 1947. Both are great-great-grandchildren of Queen Victoria. Their nine-foot-high, four-tiered wedding cake was larger than the cake that was made for the wedding of Queen Victoria and Prince Albert in 1840. Pieces of Victoria and Albert's cake have recently been on display at Windsor Castle.

Why do a bride and groom exchange rings?

Originally only the groom gave the bride a ring. The exchange of rings is a fairly recent custom. Wedding rings go back to ancient Egypt. The groom places a ring on the third finger (next to the little finger) of the bride's left hand because it was believed an artery connected that finger directly to the heart. A Roman bridegroom would send an iron ring to his bride the night before the wedding as a symbol of the strength of their union. Sometimes the Roman ring had a tiny key welded to one side as a sign

47

that the wife now owned half of her husband's wealth. Rings have always been thought to have mystic powers, and the magic could be enhanced with inscriptions.

The wedding ring has not always been worn on the middle finger of the left hand. Some people wore it on the thumb. Others wore it on right hand. Still others wore it on a string around the neck. During the years of Oliver Cromwell's Puritan rule in England, wedding rings were banned.

Gold has always been the favoured metal for wedding rings because it is precious and does not tarnish.

QUICKIES
Did you know ...

• that in Algeria, a betrothed woman wears a ring of white gold, and at the wedding the groom gives her a ring of yellow gold?

Why do some weddings have a ring-bearer carry the wedding ring on a small pillow?

In the Middle Ages, a king or queen did not wear a crown at all times. On occasions that called for the monarch to be in full regalia, the crown would be ceremoniously brought out on a satin or silk pillow carried by a page boy. At a wedding, the bride was the most important person, and was entitled to be treated like a queen. Therefore her ring might be brought out as though it were a royal crown.

How did throwing confetti become a wedding custom?

Because the main purpose of marriage was to produce children, ancient peoples showered the new bride with fertility symbols such as wheat grain. The Romans baked this wheat into small cakes for the couple, to be eaten in a tradition known as *conferriatio*, or "eating together." The guests then threw handfuls of a mixture of honeyed nuts and dried fruits called *confetto* at the bride, which we copy by throwing confetti. Many churches today discourage the throwing of confetti because of the mess it makes.

Why are flowers used as wedding decorations?

Flowers and other plants have long been associated with fertility. Roman brides carried stalks of grain. Roses have been symbols of love and beauty for centuries. However, it was not until the nineteenth century that churches were decorated with flowers for weddings,

> **QUICKIES**
> **Did you know ...**
>
> • that a ton of ore must be mined to find enough gold for one wedding ring?
> • that today the average marriage lasts 9.3 years?
> • that couples who marry in January, February, and March tend to have the highest divorce rates?
> • that two out of three couples stay together through ten years of marriage? Less than half make it through twenty-five years together.

and brides began to carry floral bouquets. Orange blossoms were often used for weddings because they were believed to bring good luck. Rosemary, which was believed to enhance memory, was used at weddings to ensure that the married couple would not forget their vows.

What is the origin of the red carpet?

Ancient people believed that evil spirits were everywhere, including in the ground. They were afraid that during a wedding, these demons would try very hard to do harm to the bride and groom. The couple was provided with a carpet to walk and stand on as protection from evil spirits in the ground. Red was considered an especially powerful colour, and because it was bright the bride and groom could clearly see it and would not make the mistake of stepping off it.

Why do guests sign a wedding book?

At one time it was required that all wedding guests sign a book to show they were present at the wedding. They were all potential witnesses in case the legitimacy of the marriage should ever be questioned.

What is the origin of "toasting" the bride and groom?

The custom of drinking to someone's health began with the ancient Greeks. A host would take his guest's cup of wine, hold it up in plain view, and then take a sip before giving it back. This was to show that the wine wasn't poisoned. In late seventeenth-century France people began to add a piece of spiced toast to the wine. A gentleman would hold up his cup of wine and say the name of the lady to whom he was drinking — or in the case of a wedding, the name of the bride. Supposedly the lady's name would enhance the flavour of the wine.

Seven Traditional Wedding Gifts for Good Luck

- Wales — love spoons
- England — bobbins for making lace
- Iceland — a carved spool for thread
- South Africa — white beads
- The Netherlands — a coin in a knotted shawl
- Hungary — money hidden in an apple
- Germany — decorated slippers

What was the most expensive wedding on record?

In May 1981 Mohammed, son of Shaik Rashid Bin Saeed Al Maktoum, married Princess Salama in Dubai, United

Arab Emirates. The wedding ceremony lasted seven days and cost forty-four million dollars.

Why do guests at wedding banquets tap spoons on dishes to make the bride and groom get up and kiss?

This custom is partly a leftover from the old practice of playing pranks on the newlyweds. Also, for many centuries the marriage has been sealed with a kiss. People in ancient times would make noise to keep evil spirits from spoiling this intimate part of the ceremony. Today, many bridal couples find it annoying when guests persist in tapping spoons, and will often ask the best man — who is usually master of ceremonies — to request that the guests not overdo the spoon tapping, or abstain from it entirely.

Why do church bells ring at a wedding?

Church bells have been rung at weddings since medieval times. Back then church bells were used to summon people to mass, to mark curfew, and to celebrate important events. One particular order of bell ringing was called the spurring bell, and this announced the third reading of the banns. Bell ringing also accompanied the procession to the church. In pre-Christian times wedding celebrants made a lot of noise to frighten away evil spirits.

The Wedding Night

What was "the right of the first night"?

In medieval times, when peasants married, the lord of the manor had the legal right to take the bride into his bed on the wedding night. In the morning he sent her, deflowered, back to her husband. Some historians say this practice was not as widespread as is commonly believed. However, the new husband was expected to pay his lord for permission to marry, and the clergyman for performing the ceremony. If the peasant could not afford to pay, he might be obliged to lend his bride to both the lord and the clergyman.

Why did men insist on their brides being virgins?

Even before the belief developed that sex before marriage was sinful, men desired virgin brides because they wanted to be sure that any children born to the marriage were in fact theirs. In some societies, such as ancient Athens, young unmarried women were absolutely forbidden to be alone in a room with any male except a close relative. A woman suspected of being briefly alone with a man, even if she were untouched, was considered damaged merchandise. There was also a lot of mysticism surrounding the state of virginity. For some people it was practically sacred. Among other beliefs, people thought sleeping with a virgin could rejuvenate an elderly man.

What does the Bible say about non-virgin brides?

The Book of Deuteronomy says that if a man discovers that his bride is not a virgin, "the men of her city shall stone her with stones that she die." Some fundamentalist Muslims believe that a girl who loses her virginity before marriage — even if she has been raped — must be killed by a male relative for shaming her family.

What cultures required someone other than the groom to sleep with the bride on the wedding night, and why?

In some groups such as the Inuit, a shaman was the first man to have intercourse with the new bride. Among the Aborigines of central Australia, a man in the bride's family had the duty of taking her virginity. Her maternal grandfather had first priority. If he was not available, or was unable to do it, the job went to a cousin on the bride's mother's side. This was because of strong superstitions concerning the blood from the broken hymen. A man who did not have the magic protection of a shaman or an elder might be rendered impotent if he got that blood on his body.

How was the bridal bed used in the wedding?

A great deal of ceremony surrounded the bridal bed. The bride and groom would lead a procession to the bed chamber, and after they had prepared for bed, everyone would crowd into the room. The priest would bless the bed before the couple got in it. Once in bed, the bride and groom would have their first marital kiss. Then they would drink a bowl of spiced or sweetened wine called "posset." Two of the groomsmen and two of the bridesmaids would sit on the sides of the bed with their backs to the centre. They would toss stockings belonging to the bride and groom over their shoulders, hoping to hit the bride or groom on the head. A hit meant the thrower would be married within the year. Then the bed curtains would be drawn and the newlyweds left alone. In some places it was customary for the groom to display a bloodstained sheet from the window to show that the marriage had been consummated, and that the bride had indeed been a virgin.

What is an "epithalamium"?

An "epithalamium" is a song or poem that celebrates a wedding. In Greek and Roman times epithalamiums were

A Surviving Fragment
of an Epithalamium
by Sappho

Bride, full of rosy love desires:
Bride, the most beautiful ornament of
Aphrodite of Paphos,
Go to your marriage-bed,
Go to the marriage-couch whereon you shall
play so gently
and sweetly with your bridegroom;
and may the evening star lead you willingly
to that place,
for there you will be astonished at the silver-
throned Hera.

sung outside the bridal chamber (*thalamus* in Greek) by young men and women, usually accompanied by soft music. The Greek poet Sappho and the Roman poet Catallus were famous composers of epithalamiums. Such writers were often commissioned to write wedding songs for aristocratic families. In 1874 Walt Whitman wrote an epithalamium titled "A Kiss for the Bride" for President Ulysses S. Grant's daughter Nellie.

What were "fescennine songs"?

"Fescennine songs" date back to ancient Rome. Unlike the romantic epithalamium, a fescennine song was a lewd take on what was happening in the bridal chamber. It was not necessarily a prank to embarrass the newlyweds; people believed these rude songs distracted the evil spirits who might otherwise harm the married couple. Therefore, the more shocking the lyrics, the better.

A Not-Too-Racy Excerpt from a Fescennine Poem by Catallus

He married himself a girl, a regular flower in bloom,
A girl tender and delicious, a frisky little lamb,
To be guarded real careful, like your juiciest grapes.

What is the origin of the "shivaree"?

A "shivaree" (or "charivari") is a noisy mock serenade of a couple on their wedding night. Wedding guests, often after much alcohol has been consumed, will stand outside the house where the couple are spending their first night together and sing naughty songs. This prank actually began in medieval times as a punishment called *charivaris* or "rough songs." If the people of a community did not approve of a wedding match, they would surround the house and make noise with anything available. They might also hang the offending persons in effigy, or beat straw dummies. The *charivaris* was also used to publicly shame people suspected of sexual misconduct and men who were known to be wife beaters. It eventually changed to a form of crude celebration.

Just Married

Why do wedding celebrants honk car horns as they drive from the church to the reception hall?

This goes back to the ancient practice of making noise to frighten away evil spirits. For much of the twentieth century it was common for blaring car horns to let people know a couple had just been married. However, in many communities there are now by-laws that prohibit excessive noise, and wedding celebrants who blow their car horns too enthusiastically are liable to be fined.

What is the origin of the honeymoon trip?

One source says that after a bride had eloped, or been carried off, the couple would go away for a while to give the enraged father of the bride time to cool off. In the nineteenth century, newlyweds would take a "bridal tour" so they could meet family members who had been unable to attend the wedding. Newly wedded couples eventually began to choose destinations that would allow them more privacy than visits to the homes of relatives.

Why is it called a "honeymoon"?

Four thousand years ago, in ancient Babylon, for a full lunar month the father of the bride supplied his son-in-law with plenty of mead. Mead is an alcoholic beverage made from honey. This period was called the "honey month." The word "honeymoon" did not come into English usage until 1546. At that time, very few people could afford a honeymoon vacation.

How did Niagara Falls become the "honeymoon capital" of the world?

Niagara Falls, shared by Canada and the United States, is one of North America's oldest tourist destinations. By the mid-nineteenth century it had become a cultural icon. Everybody who was anybody visited the Falls. Poets wrote odes to the Falls. There were wonderful legends, such as the mythical tale of the Maid of the Mist. Sharp-minded entrepreneurs capitalized on the popularity of the

Falls and presented the site as the perfect place to spend a honeymoon. They pitched it as the place where "the faithful lover may return ... with ever-new delight, ever-growing affection."

What was the "Niagara Honeymoon Song"?

The song was part of a late-1940s promotional campaign to present Niagara Falls as a honeymoon destination. Other gimmicks were "honeymoon certificates" and "community showers" for lucky couples. The song went, in part:

> See Niagara's waters rolling
> See the misty spray
> See the happy lovers strolling
> It's everybody's wedding day

What famous Irish writer was not impressed with Niagara Falls?

Oscar Wilde, who visited Niagara in 1882, referred to the Falls as "simply a vast unnecessary volume of water going the wrong way and then falling over unnecessary rocks." Pressed to say something good about the Falls, Wilde continued, "The wonder would be if the water did not fall! Every American bride is taken there, and the sight of the stupendous waterfall must be one of the earliest, if not the keenest, disappointments in American married life." Wilde also allegedly said that Niagara Falls must be "the second greatest disappointment" in American married life. In spite of Wilde's cynical remarks, his brother William took his bride to Niagara Falls in 1891.

What advice did "sex experts" of the early twentieth century have for honeymooners?

Honeymooners were advised not to have sex on their first night as man and wife. The sex experts said that after all the activity and stress of the wedding, the newlyweds — especially the bride — would be too fatigued for sex. Also the bridegroom, in his passion, was liable to be brutish. Far better, said the sex experts, to wait until the second night when the bride would be more rested, and the bridegroom more likely to control his aggressive urges.

What was "honeymoon shock"?

In the early twentieth century, doctors warned that newlyweds who were not properly prepared for their first honeymoon night could suffer "honeymoon shock." According to these doctors, women who had bad honeymoon sexual experiences could develop a painful condition called *vaginismus*. Men who had similar bad experiences could be rendered impotent for life. Doctors recommended that young people about to be married go to their doctors for a detailed, clinical explanation about sexual intercourse.

What were "honeymoon postcards"?

Honeymoon postcards were popular in the mid-twentieth century, and were usually available in honeymoon hotspots like Niagara Falls. They typically featured cartoon drawings of a beautiful bride and a panting groom, with sexually suggestive captions like, "She got him today; he'll get her tonight," or "Getting married is like buying a car. Once you get the licence, you can go as far as you like."

QUICKIES
Did you know ...

• that the automobile revolutionized the honeymoon? The car made it possible for more people to go on honeymoons, and it made far more places available to honeymooners. Automobile clubs even offer special honeymoon packages. A new type of accommodation called the "motor hotel," or "motel," suddenly appeared. The motel was attractive not only to honeymooners and traveling salesmen, but also to people involved in illicit affairs.

Where are the most popular honeymoon destinations today?

According to a survey taken in 2007 by a magazine called *Modern Bride*, the top five honeymoon destinations for that year were:

> Italy
> Hawaii
> Tahiti
> Costa Rica
> Mexico

Leave a Ladder under the Window

How would elopers get around the law requiring the publication of banns?

Unscrupulous clergymen would, for a price, publish the banns three times and perform the marriage, all on the same day. In some places the fugitive lovers would simply have the knot tied by a justice of the peace.

How did Lord Hardwick's Marriage Act of 1754 attempt to discourage people from eloping?

The act declared that: "all marriages solemnized from and

QUICKIES
Did you know ...

• that Juliet is only thirteen years old when she meets Romeo? However, her age is not an issue. Her father is already in the process of arranging a marriage for her. In Shakespearean times, girls could be married at the age of twelve, and boys at fourteen.

after March 25, 1754, in any other place than a church or such publick chapel, unless by special license as aforesaid, or that shall be solemnized without publication of banns or license of marriage from a person or persons having authority to grant the same first had and obtained, shall be null and void to all intents and purposes whatsoever."

What was a "Fleet marriage"?

Fleet Prison was a notorious debtor's prison in London. It was the centre of the very lucrative "irregular" marriage trade. Persons wishing to marry secretly — for whatever reason — would go to Fleet Prison or one of the churches in its neighbourhood. The prison itself was outside the jurisdiction of the church, and so could ignore ecclesiastical rules regarding weddings. Corrupt wardens and clergymen in Fleet Prison and its environs would marry anyone to anyone, regardless of age or social standing. It did not even matter if one of the participants was already married. Many of the marriages were performed by clergymen who had been defrocked, or were imposters who had never been ordained. In the mid-eighteenth century over half of all London weddings were Fleet marriages.

Why was Gretna Green important to elopers?

Gretna Green, Scotland, was just across the border from England. Lord Hardwick's Marriage Act did not apply to Scotland, so many eloping English couples went there to get married.

Who had the most severe punishments for elopement?

The people who had the strongest objections to elopement may have been the aboriginal tribes of Australia. Couples who eloped had to stay away for years. If they returned too soon they would be severely punished and any children would be killed. When the offending couple did finally return, they would have to buy their way back into favour with gifts of food for the husband's parents.

Where is elopement the preferred form of marriage?

In the rural parts of Burma (also called Myanmar) and

among the large numbers of urban poor, elopement is the favourite practice for marriage. Most people simply cannot afford the cost of a wedding.

Why do young lovers in Tuvalu often elope?

In this tiny, South Pacific island nation, a young man's parents have the final say in whether or not the girl he wants to marry is acceptable. In many communities courting is forbidden. Young men and women meet in the presence of a chaperone called a *fei fekau*. There is a more dangerous courting practice called *moetolo*, which means "sleep crawl," in which the young man sneaks into the young woman's house at night when the rest of her family is asleep. If the trespasser is caught, he can be punished. Many young people today simply turn their backs on tradition and elope.

What classic love story is centred around an elopement?

Shakespeare's *Romeo and Juliet*. Literature's most famous star-crossed lovers come from feuding families that would never agree to their marriage. The couple therefore slip away to be married in secret.

Twelve Famous People Who Eloped, and Who They Ran Off With

- Betsy Ross (nee Griscom), American patriot: John Ross
- Robert Browning, British poet: Elizabeth Barrett
- Judith of Flanders, Frankish princess: Count Baldwin Iron Arm
- Peter Abelard, French philosopher: Heloise
- Kirk Douglas, American actor: Anne Buydens
- Gene Tierney, American actress: Oleg Cassini
- Yoko Ono, Japanese artist: Toshi Ichiyanagi
- Janet Jackson, American recording artist: James Debarge
- Jack Black, American actor: Tanya Haden
- Devika Rani, Indian actress: Jeevan Naiya Najam-ul-Hussain
- James Donnelly, Irish-Canadian farmer (of Black Donnelly notoriety): Johannah McGee
- Michael Jackson, recording artist: Lisa Marie Presley

Wedding Superstitions

What are some ways of ensuring good luck for the newly married couple?

- A harvest moon shining on the wedding bed will make the marriage fruitful.
- The couple will prosper if the bride has a gold or silver coin in her shoe.
- If a chimney sweep makes an appearance at your wedding, complete with sooty clothes and dirty face, it will bring good luck, but you must pay the boy.
- It will bring good luck if the newlyweds sleep with their heads pointed north. It is also lucky if the bride is the first to put her bare feet on the floor in the morning.

- Good fortune will shine on the marriage if the bride's sister or nearest female relative makes up the wedding bed on the wedding day. It will also bring good fortune if the groom and two of his groomsmen sleep in the wedding bed the night before the wedding. Nail a gold or silver coin to the foot of the marriage bed and prosperity is practically guaranteed.

- Wrap a pound of limburger cheese in two towels and put it under a pillow of the wedding bed on the first night, and the couple will have good fortune and a large family.

- It will bring good luck to the marriage if the groom pays the clergyman with an odd sum of money.

- Seeing a black cat, lamb, spider, frog, or rainbow on the way to the ceremony are all indications of good luck.

- Throwing old shoes after the newlyweds as they depart for the honeymoon will ensure them a safe and happy trip.

> **QUICKIES**
> **Did you know ...**
>
> • that in Aruba a newly married woman must steal her husband's right sock and, before midnight on the third Monday of the month, bury it to the right of the main door of the house? This will keep him from wandering.

What things mean bad luck for a marriage?

Bad luck in one form or another will plague the married couple if:

- the groom sees the bride within the twenty-four-hour period before the wedding,
- either the bride or groom drops the ring during the ceremony,
- they sleep in their new home on the wedding night,
- the bride puts her bare feet on the floor before getting into the wedding bed,
- they find a flea in the bed,
- the bride or groom trips over the threshold while entering their new home, or enters with the left foot first,
- the bride or groom see an open grave, a pig, a lizard, or hear a crow on the way to the ceremony,
- the bride's veil is accidentally torn,
- the bride or groom see a monk or a nun before the ceremony, because those people are associated with poverty,
- the wedding ring is too tight — one partner in the marriage will stifle the other and the marriage will be spoiled by jealousy. If the wedding ring is too loose, the marriage will be broken by infidelity,
- the bride makes her own wedding dress, or tries it on before the wedding day.

What animal is most associated with bringing good luck to a marriage?

Oddly enough, considering it is so often associated with bad luck and witchcraft, the black cat is believed to bring good luck to young women in search of a husband, and to newlyweds. If the bride or groom sees a black cat on the way to or from the church, they will have a happy marriage. If the bride hears a black cat sneeze on her wedding day, that too means good luck. In some places the bride is given a symbolic black cat charm to carry during the wedding ceremony.

Weddings in Literature, Movies, TV, and History

How did a wedding lead to the Trojan War?

The gods and goddesses of ancient Greece were celebrating the wedding of the goddess Thetis to the hero Peleus. The goddess Eris (Discordia to the Romans) was not invited because she was a troublemaker. Eris made a dramatic appearance at the wedding feast and cast down a golden apple that was inscribed with the words, "For the Fairest." Hera, Athena, and Aphrodite immediately began to quarrel over who should have the apple. The dispute was eventually settled by Paris, a prince of Troy, who awarded the apple to Aphrodite. She, however, had bribed Paris by offering him the most beautiful woman in the world. This was Helen of Sparta, wife of King Menelaus. When Paris abducted Helen and took her to Troy, the Greeks besieged the city.

Who was Hymenaios?

In Greek mythology Hymen was the god of marriage. It is not certain if the female virgin's hymen was named after him, or he was named after it. He presided over all of the weddings of the gods, and his presence at human weddings was essential. Otherwise, the marriage was doomed. Before an ancient Greek wedding, children would run around calling his name to be sure the god would be at the wedding. One story says he was a son of Apollo and a nymph; another says his parents were Bacchus and Aphrodite. Yet another legend says he was a poor Athenian youth who fell in love with a beautiful aristocratic girl, but could not speak to her because of her social status. However, after he courageously rescued her from a gang of bandits, they were married and lived happily ever after. Athenians therefore honoured his name at all weddings by singing lyric poems called "hymeneals." ("Hymeneal" is the forerunner of the modern word "hymn.")

Runaway Brides (and Grooms!) – Eight Movies in which Someone Gets Ditched at the Altar

- *While You Were Sleeping* (1995, starring Sandra Bullock and Bill Pullman)
- *Smokey and the Bandit* (1977, starring Burt Reynolds and Sally Field)
- *Runaway Bride* (1999, starring Julia Roberts and Richard Gere)
- *Arthur* (1981, starring Dudley Moore and Liza Minnelli)
- *The Wedding Singer* (1998, starring Adam Sandler and Drew Barrymore)
- *The Wedding Planner* (2001, starring Jennifer Lopez and Matthew McConaughey)
- *The Graduate* (1967, starring Dustin Hoffman, Katharine Ross, and Anne Bancroft)
- *Wayne's World 2* (1993, starring Mike Myers and Tia Carrere)

What biblical king demanded one hundred foreskins as a bride price?

After the young Hebrew shepherd David killed the Philistine giant, Goliath, he asked for Michal, the daughter of King Saul, in marriage. Saul did not want David for a son-in-law, but he couldn't turn the hero down directly. So he told David he must pay a bride price of one hundred Philistine foreskins. Of course, he was hoping David would be killed trying to collect the foreskins. However, David was successful, and Saul had to agree to the wedding.

What were "Tobias nights"?

Tobias is the central character in the Book of Tobit, a book of the Old Testament that is in the Catholic Bible, but is dismissed as apocryphal by the Protestant churches. In the land of Media there lives a woman named Sarah who has been married seven times. Each of her husbands died in the bridal chamber on their wedding night. Their deaths were caused by a demon named Asmodeus. Tobias falls in love with Sarah, but an angel warns him of what happened to his predecessors. On their wedding night, Tobias and Sarah do not consummate their marriage. Instead, Tobias burns the heart and liver of a fish, and the fumes drive Asmodeus away. Having survived the deadly wedding night, Tobias lives happily ever after with Sarah.

People who took the story as fact would abstain from sex not only on their wedding night, but for two or three nights just to be safe. These first chaste nights of marriage were called "Tobias nights."

Who is probably English literature's most famous jilted bride?

In Charles Dickens' novel *Great Expectations,* the protagonist, Pip, meets the very wealthy and very strange Miss Havisham. Many years earlier Miss Havisham was left standing at the altar by a man she loved, but who turned out to be a scoundrel. At the time she comes into Pip's life, Miss Havisham lives in a crumbling old mansion and is still wearing her wedding dress, now yellow with age. The rotting wedding decorations still hang from the walls, and the dried out remains of the wedding cake are on the table. Miss Havisham has made up her mind to have revenge on all men.

How did a riddle ruin the wedding feast of the Old Testament hero, Samson?

Even before he met the treacherous Delilah, Samson had a weakness for Philistine women, and had resolved to marry one — Timnah — even though the Philistines were the enemies of his own people. At the wedding feast, attended by thirty Philistine men, Samson posed a riddle: "Out of the eater came forth food, and out of the strong came forth sweetness." In Samson's absence the Philistines forced his bride to tell them the answer — the riddle referred to Samson's victory over a lion (the "eater"), in whose carcass there was a swarm of bees and honey. When the Philistines confronted Samson with the answer, he said they had "plowed my heifer" for the answer, but he had to pay the wager of a cloak for each man. This was the beginning of Samson's one-man war against the Philistines.

What popular television series began with a runaway bride dropping by a coffee shop?

In the pilot for *Friends*, Rachel Green, wearing a wedding dress, tracks down her old friend Monica and asks for a place to stay. Rachel has just left her husband at the altar after realizing he looks "like Mr. Potato Head."

Eight Famous Fictional Made-for-TV Weddings

- Luke Spencer and Laura Webber on *General Hospital*
- Orson Hodge and Bree Van de Kamp on *Desperate Housewives*
- Chandler Bing and Monica Geller on *Friends*
- Zach Morris and Kelly Kapowski on *Saved by the Bell: Wedding in Las Vegas*
- Chachi Arcola and Joanie Cunningham on *Happy Days*
- Niles Crane and Daphne Moon on *Frasier*
- David Silver and Donna Martin on *Beverley Hills, 90210*
- Marsha Brady to Wally Logan and Jan Brady to Philip Covington III on *The Brady Girls Get Married*

What was significant about the wedding at Cana?

According to the Gospel of John, Jesus and his mother attended a wedding at Cana. The host ran out of wine. At his mother's request, Jesus ordered some vats to be filled with water, which he then turned into wine. Guests remarked that the host had saved the best wine for the last. This was the first of the miracles attributed to Jesus.

What is Sadie Hawkins Day?

Al Capp, creator of the *Li'l Abner* comic strip, introduced his readers to Sadie Hawkins Day on

November 15, 1937, and it quickly became an American institution. The residents of Dogpatch, Abner Yokum's hometown, held an annual footrace in which the unmarried women tried to chase down the bachelors. If a woman caught a man and dragged him over the finish line

Five Famous "Real" Made-for-TV Weddings

- Rick Rockwell and Darva Conger on *Who Wants to Marry a Multimillionaire*
- Ryan Setter and Trista Rehn from *The Bachelorette* on *Trista and Ryan's Wedding*
- Reality stars Rob Mariano and Amber Brkich on *Rob and Amber Get Married*
- Tiny Tim and Miss Vicki on *The Tonight Show*
- Christopher Knight and Adrianne Curry on *My Fair Brady*

And One "Semi-Real" Made-for-TV Wedding

- Randy "Macho Man" Savage and Miss Elizabeth on *WWF Summerslam 1991*. (The pair had been married in real life since 1984.)

before sundown, he had to marry her. Participation in the event was compulsory, and the town's preacher, Marryin' Sam, was on hand to perform the ceremony. The race was named in honour of "the homeliest gal in the hills." Sadie Hawkins Day dances, in which the girls asked the boys for dates and people dressed like hillbillies, became very popular in the United States and Canada. Sadie Hawkins Day events are still held in some parts of the United States.

What is the highest-grossing wedding movie of all time?

My Big Fat Greek Wedding, written by and starring Nia Vardalos, has grossed more than any wedding-themed film, bringing in $241,438,208. The film began life as a one-woman stage show in Los Angeles. Tom Hanks happened to be in attendance for one performance, and was so enthralled with the show that he bought the film rights and agreed to cast Vardalos in the lead.

The theatrical success of the film is all the more remarkable when one considers that, in its opening weekend, it grossed a mere $597,362.

Who was John Nevison and what incident marred his wedding?

John Nevison was a notorious seventeenth-century

Ten of the Most Publicized Weddings of the Twentieth Century

- Edward, the Duke of Windsor to Wallis Simpson, June 3, 1937
- Prince Ranier of Monaco to Grace Kelly, April 19, 1956
- Richard Burton to Elizabeth Taylor, March 15, 1964 (again on October 10, 1975)
- Frank Sinatra to Mia Farrow, July 19, 1966
- Aristotle Onasiss to Jacqueline Kennedy, October 20, 1968
- Paul McCartney to Linda Eastman, March 12, 1969
- Tiny Tim (Herbert Khaury) to Miss Vicki (Victoria May Budinger), December 17, 1969
- Prince Charles to Lady Diana Spencer, July 12, 1981
- Wayne Gretzky to Janet Jones, July 17, 1988
- Richard Gomez to Lucy Torres, April 28, 1998

English highwayman. King Charles II nicknamed the outlaw "Swift Nicks" after he made a dramatic escape from prison. At Nevison's wedding someone placed a new twist on the old custom of breaking a wedding cake over the bride's head by breaking what is politely called a cow-pie over her head.

Where were brides traditionally "abducted" in colonial America?

In eighteenth-century Connecticut, after the wedding a gr-oup of young men would "kidnap" the bride and take her to a tavern. The groom and his friends would ride after them to "rescue" the girl. When they reached the tavern the groom ransomed the bride by buying food and drinks for everyone.

Where was a practice modern people consider incestuous common among the social elite?

Among the royal families and aristocracy of ancient Egypt, marriage between brothers and sisters, and even parents and children, was not only tolerated, but was sometimes obligatory. It was seen as a method of keeping bloodlines pure.

Ten Famous People
Who Married Their Cousins

- Johann Sebastian Bach, German composer: married Barbara Bach
- Albert Einstein, German scientist: married Elsa Lowenthal Einstein
- Charles Darwin, British naturalist: married Emma Wedgewood
- Thomas Jefferson, American president: married Martha Wayles
- Edgar Allan Poe, American author: married Virginia Clemm
- H.G. Wells, British author: married Isabel Mary Wells
- John A. Macdonald, Canadian prime minister: married Isabella Clark
- Jesse James, American outlaw: married Zerelda Simms
- Jerry Lee Lewis, American recording artist: married Myra Gayle Brown
- Elizabeth II, British monarch: married Philip Mountbatten

Weddings around the World

Where are "bride's tears" served?

Weddings in the Netherlands are known for the quantities of food and drink served. There is a traditional sweetmeat called "bride's sugar" and a spiced wine called "bride's tears."

What is unique about a Peruvian wedding cake?

There are numerous coloured ribbons attached to a Peruvian wedding cake. One of the ribbons is attached to a ring. Unmarried female wedding guests take turns pulling the ribbons. The one who gets the ring is believed to be the next person to get married.

How does a certain Malaysian wedding custom make the ceremony somewhat resemble an Easter celebration?

At a Malaysian wedding the bride and groom distribute brightly decorated hard-boiled eggs to the guests. These are symbols of fertility. The groom gives the bride trays full of food and money folded into the shapes of animals and flowers.

What is the traditional wedding drink in certain parts of Madagascar?

Malagasy wedding celebrations are usually lavish, with a lot of food. In some

QUICKIES
Did you know ...

• that the brides and grooms at Carib weddings spoke different languages? The Carib Indians, for whom the Caribbean was named, were fierce warriors who raided other native peoples for brides. The Carib men spoke their own language, but the reluctant brides spoke the languages of whatever groups they were kidnapped away from. The Caribs were also cannibals. Any men or boys they captured were eaten.

parts of Madagascar a cow is slaughtered during the wedding ceremony. The bride and groom and all of the guests are obliged to drink the cow's blood.

How is the bride dressed in a traditional Norwegian wedding?

In a traditional Norwegian wedding the bride wears white or silver. She also wears a crown that has several spoon-shaped danglers hanging from it. These are supposed to keep away evil spirits. The bridesmaids are similarly dressed, to further confuse the demons. The groom wears a traditional costume called a *bunad*.

Where are guns used to announce important events like weddings?

In the mountains of Albania, announcements of important events such as weddings, births, and deaths are passed from one house or community to another by means of a gunshot or a shout that echoes across the valleys. Albanian wedding celebrations are known for being especially noisy.

Why do men in Kyrgyzstan still engage in marriage by capture?

Many men in this former republic of the Soviet Union continue to practice a custom called *ala Kachuu,* which literally means "grab and run." A man who either cannot find a woman who is willing to marry him, or who does not want to pay the costs of courtship and a bride price, will simply abduct a woman and force her into marriage. The practice has been illegal for many years, but about half the Kyrgyz weddings that take place each year are the result of *ala Kachuu.* Authorities find it difficult to abolish the practice because Kyrgyz males consider it a manly act.

How are the bride and groom "tested" after a traditional Czech wedding?

When a Czech groom takes his bride to their new home after the wedding, he finds an axe and a bottle of wine at the threshold. If he picks up the axe first, it means he will be a hard worker and a good husband. If he picks up the wine first, he will be a drunkard. In the house there is a broom in one corner. If the bride sees it and swiftly cleans the house, she will be a good housewife. If she does not, she will be a lazy housewife.

How does a suitor in Fiji show the father of his prospective bride that he is worthy of her?

Among the people of Fiji it is customary for a young man to ask the girl's father for her hand in marriage. He is also expected to present the father with a valuable present to show that he has status and wealth. Traditionally, the gift is a whale's tooth. It is also up to the groom to provide a lavish wedding feast.

When does the greatest number of Irish weddings take place?

In Ireland the luckiest day on which to be married is, of course, St. Patrick's Day. However, a traditional Irish bride wears blue, because that is considered a lucky colour. She will also braid her hair because that brings good luck and helps preserve her power as a woman.

QUICKIES
Did you know ...

• that in Hungary the bride smashes a plate on the floor? The more pieces the plate breaks into, the more successful the marriage will be.

What is unusual about an Armenian wedding?

At a traditional wedding in Armenia, the bride wears a red silk gown and a cardboard headpiece that is shaped like wings and decorated with feathers. During the marriage ceremony two white doves symbolizing love and happiness are released. In the last dance of the wedding festivities, the *Mom bar,* the celebrants carry lit candles. When the dance is over the candles are extinguished as a sign that it is time for everybody to go home.

How do brides in the Dominican Republic seek special blessing on their wedding day?

The population of this Caribbean nation is almost entirely Roman Catholic. During the wedding ceremony, which is usually done according to Catholic traditions, the bride will present roses to a statue of the Virgin Mary before she and the groom are pronounced man and wife. This is done in hope that the Virgin will bestow her blessing on the marriage.

What is a "wedding towel"?

In Belarus the wedding towel has been part of the traditional marriage ceremony since ancient times. In the early days of the tradition, the bride and groom would stand on a towel during the ritual. Then the bride would drag the towel around the altar, marking the way for young women who were still unmarried to follow her into matrimony. Today in Belarus, wedding gifts are wrapped in colourful towels.

Where is a symbolic fight part of the wedding celebration?

In Kenya, wedding ceremonies vary from tribe to tribe. Among the Masai, a traditional wedding celebration includes a symbolic fight between the families of the bride and groom. This may be a leftover from the days when brides were captured on raids. In some instances the female relatives of the groom verbally abuse the bride. This is not done out of malice, but to protect her from evil spirits.

Why do men in China tend to marry later than men in other countries?

In Chinese culture it is important to display wealth and prosperity. Weddings are expected to be lavish and expensive, otherwise the families involved are shamed. Therefore, a man has to be able to save enough money to put on a grand wedding. Even for wealthy men this can be a challenge, because socially prominent people are expected to have very ostentatious weddings.